Grief Changed Me—So Did Grace

Grief rewrote my story, but grace helped me hold the pen.

Grief Changed Me—So Did Grace

Grief Changed Me—So Did Grace
Finding Strength during Loss

Delilah Klug

Grief Changed Me—So Did Grace

Grief Changed Me—So Did Grace

Preface

I didn't set out to write a book. I set out to survive.

After losing my husband, I found myself standing in a world that no longer made sense.

The life I had known shattered. I was left to pick up the pieces of a reality I couldn't quite recognize.

In the chaos, I turned to writing—first as a silent release, then as an act of surrender.

This book was born from grief, yes—but it grew into something more. It's about love—the kind that never fades.

About learning to breathe again when the world has stopped turning. About finding the strength to live, even when you don't know how.

If you're holding this book, know this: You are not alone. Grief has changed you, but grace can change you too.

These words are fragments of my heart. They offer the truth that healing is not linear, that strength sometimes takes the form of tears, and that hope can still find a way—even in the darkest of places.

Grief Changed Me—So Did Grace

DEDICATION

For My Husband

I lost you far too soon.
Yet your love, your strength, and your memory have never left me.
You are my miracle, my reminder, my reason to keep moving forward.
This book holds my pain, but it also holds my love for you.
Each page carries the hope that you are still with me—
Still guiding me, still lifting me,
Still reminding me to never give up.
I miss you endlessly.
Love you forever.

For My Children

You were my reason to keep going when everything inside me wanted
to stop.
Your laughter pierced through the silence of my grief.
Your hugs held me together when I felt like I was falling apart.
You didn't just witness my healing—you helped create it.
This book is for you,
Because your love helped me find light in the darkest of places.
Thank you for reminding me that even in loss, life can still be beautiful.

Grief Changed Me—So Did Grace

CONTENTS

Grief Changed Me—So Did Grace

ACKNOWLEDGMENTS

To my children—

Thank you for being the light I needed when the world felt impossibly dark.

Your laughter gave me reasons to keep going.
Your resilience reminded me that healing was still possible.

This book exists because of you—because your love helped me find grace during grief.

We didn't just survive—we healed together, step by step, breath by breath.

I love you more than words will ever be able to say.

Grief Changed Me—So Did Grace

Grief Changed Me—So Did Grace

1 THE STORM

Nothing could have prepared me for this—
the deep fall,
the countless times I felt shattered,
before I found the strength to stand again.

But what's truly extraordinary—
is the way you keep finding your feet.

I was a wife,
a mother holding together a home—
a place filled with the rhythm of everyday life—
a teenage son learning to spread his wings,
a little girl still needing bedtime stories.

Then, in a single, breath-stealing moment,
the noise of my life collapsed into silence—
a quiet so profound, it felt endless.

The life we knew was gone.
I was left standing in the ashes—
caught in the eye of the storm I never saw coming,
trying to navigate a world that had lost all its familiar meaning.

Grief Changed Me—So Did Grace

In those early days,
grief felt like a storm—
crushing, relentless, all-consuming.

I walked through the world carrying invisible wounds,
while those around me expected life to continue—
as if I hadn't just survived the unthinkable.

The pieces of what remained felt too shattered,
too foreign,
for me to grasp.

**When was the last time a wave of grief took over,
and how did you survive it?**

Grief Changed Me—So Did Grace

I remember the numbness most of all.
It wasn't sadness at first—
but a deep, paralyzing disbelief.

How could someone I loved so much—
be gone?!

We all have that feeling—
If I could've given you my last breath, I would have.

That line makes time stand still,
forever lost in that moment.

It hurt to breathe without you.
Each inhale scorched my lungs—
who knew something as simple as breathing
could hurt this deeply?

How could everything I once loved,
cherished,
and valued—
now lie in the ashes at my feet?

Grief Changed Me—So Did Grace

Shock will paralyze you—
fog your mind,
warp your sense of reality,
like standing in a world that is unrecognizable.

So many thoughts will consume you—
your mind,
your memory,
your every breath.

You'll forget a lot of things
after experiencing a sudden, traumatic loss—
it's your mind and body's way of protecting you.

It won't make sense at first—
why you can't remember such precious memories.

The sheer mental strain it takes to survive a loss like this
is something most friends and family can't truly comprehend.

The world around me felt too loud,
but the space I was left in
felt too quiet.

Grief Changed Me—So Did Grace

There was a quiet before the storm—
a peace I never took for granted,
a life I held close,
never imagining how quickly it could all slip away.

The walls that once echoed with shared laughter,
the rooms that held our countless memories,
now stand as silent witnesses to a life forever changed.

My soul—
crushed by the careless words and actions
of people who thought they were just making conversation—
never realizing how deep their words cut.

Like shards of glass slicing my skin
as I tried to escape the fire
that surrounded my world.

The first morning I woke up to his absence,
it felt like a crack had formed deep within me—
one that might never fully mend.

My heart shattered into a million pieces.
My soul felt as if it had left my body.
A silent ache that echoed through every corner of my being.

Grief Changed Me—So Did Grace

At times, the pain was so sharp,
my heart begged for any kind of comfort—
as I felt it breaking piece by piece.

The kind of comfort that might have mended it—
but it never came.

I needed to protect my heart—
and my children's hearts—
hearts that had been damaged overnight.

I couldn't speak.

The brain fog was so thick,
it swallowed my thoughts.

And when I did manage to say something,
my voice crackled—
faint,
and frayed,
fading in and out—

like a tube had been down my throat,
as if the grief had etched its presence into every breath.

Shock leaves you stunned in complete disbelief.
It's like trying to build a home without a blueprint,
with no tools,
and your hands shaking from the loss.

Grief Changed Me—So Did Grace

Making every decision by myself—
something I never imagined I'd face—
was a weight I couldn't prepare for.

Trying to grasp a single thought—
let alone hold it—
felt impossible
in those heavy, disoriented moments.

Just trying to make it through the day,
knowing you need to eat something—anything—
but you don't have an appetite.

The stress hit my body like a silent storm,
stripping me of more than just peace.

I started losing my hair—
a stark, undeniable reminder
that even my body struggled to carry the weight of this loss.

It was as if the grief had reached down to the roots of my being,
unraveling the parts of me that once felt unbreakable.

I became a fragile version of myself—
a woman standing in the wreckage,
trying to hold together the pieces of a life that no longer fit.

Grief Changed Me—So Did Grace

Every step felt unsteady,
each breath a reminder of how deeply my world had shifted.

I moved through the days in a haze,
grasping at fragments of the person I used to be,
wondering if I would ever feel whole again.

Grief takes many forms—
it touches your physical health,
your mental health,
your overall well-being.

The grief came in waves—
unpredictable,
consuming.

I questioned everything.
Was it something I missed?
Something I could've done?

Grief Changed Me—So Did Grace

The silence in the house
echoed louder than any sound—
a haunting reminder
that my life had been split in two:
the before,
and the unbearable after.

The walls around me had nothing to say.
They were new,
but hollow—
cold,
untouched by laughter or love.

They held no memories,
no echoes of the life we once lived.

Just drywall and paint
on the land where everything was lost.

A constant reminder
of all I can never get back.

Grief Changed Me—So Did Grace

Yet even in the eye of the storm,
something within me held on—
not from strength,
but because I had no other choice.

Survival became instinct.
Each breath, each tear, each whispered memory—
was a step forward, even when it felt like I was standing still.

Grief didn't ask for permission to change me.
It just did—without warning, without mercy.

Yet even as the weight of grief bore down,
something deep within me refused to surrender.

Not out of strength—
but out of the will to keep moving.

Even in the wreckage, even in the ash,
not with the roar of defiance,
but with the quiet, unspoken resolve to keep going.

Because somewhere in the ashes,
in the quiet after the storm,
I found fragments of who I once was—
and glimpses of who I might still become.

Even when the storm felt endless,
something within me kept reaching for the light,
a quiet reminder that I am more than my brokenness,
that I am still here—
still becoming.

Grief Changed Me—So Did Grace

— "You will survive the storm, and you will learn to dance in the rain." — Unknown

Grief Changed Me—So Did Grace

Journaling Your Thoughts

What moment in your grief journey felt like the fiercest storm?
Describe it in detail—what did it feel like, sound like, or even look like emotionally?

Grief Changed Me—So Did Grace

Journaling Your Thoughts

When everything felt like it was falling apart,
what (or who) helped you hold on,
even just a little?

Grief Changed Me—So Did Grace

We learn to mask our heartbreak with small talk and smiles,
even when we're barely holding it together.

Because sometimes pretending we're okay
is the only way we know how to survive the day.

But beneath the surface, our hearts still ache.
Behind every forced smile, there's a quiet, unspoken grief—
a silent scream we keep hidden for the sake of others.

A silent reminder of all that's been lost,
and the strength it takes to keep moving,
even when the weight feels unbearable.

Grief Changed Me—So Did Grace

2 BEHIND THE SMILE

There will come a time
when each of us faces the weight of profound loss—
a loss so deep it shifts the very ground beneath your feet,
leaving you wondering if you'll ever stand again.

There were so many nights I lay awake in the dark,
completely consumed by the weight of grief—
like a heavy fog pressing against my chest,
making it hard to breathe,
hard to think,
hard to be.

Grief had pulled me into a deep, dark hole—
one I dug to hide away from the world.

Grief Changed Me—So Did Grace

I needed to feel safe again.
In a world that now feels fragile and uncertain.
We see it differently now—forever changed.

After deep loss, something shifts.
You become guarded.
Every part of you goes on high alert—
cautious, protective, reactive—
like bricks stacking themselves around your heart,
quietly building a wall to shield you from more pain.

The world feels dangerous,
unpredictable,
and you begin to lose trust in everything—
even in yourself.

But even then, you find a way to smile—
to mask the cracks forming beneath the surface,
to keep moving, even as the weight builds beneath it all.

You shed the old parts of you,
the parts that once felt safe,
comfortable, and whole.

But slowly—
almost silently—
growth begins to stir,
often without you even realizing it,
whispering that you are still here.

Grief Changed Me—So Did Grace

Life had broken me,
Stolen every dream I once held for my future.

Yet, I put on a smile
and showed up the best way I could.

But over time, you notice it—
tiny cracks forming in the walls around your heart,
where light, hesitant but persistent, begins to filter in again.

But there are moments,
some days,
when the weight of it all catches up with you...

Grief never announces itself.
It creeps in silently,
slipping into everyday moments—
shopping in a store,
setting one less plate at the table—
an act so small, yet it feels like a deep betrayal,
a quiet reminder that the family once gathered there is forever changed.

The empty chair becomes more than just a seat.
It's a silent testament to what's been lost,
a reminder that the rhythm of dinner conversations is offbeat,
the laughter quieter, the silences longer.

Every meal a reminder of the void,
the unspoken absence that shifts the very air in the room.

Grief Changed Me—So Did Grace

Even the simple act of cooking after loss feels different—
the clatter of pots and pans on the gas stove echoing in a way it never
did before—
a hollow sound in a kitchen that once buzzed with music,
as we danced to his favorite songs.

Realizing I hadn't cried in days
and then suddenly feeling guilty for it.

Because you feel like you must hold it all together—
for your kids,
your family,
your coworkers.

But the truth is... you don't.

Some days, the pain is invisible to everyone but you.

Behind the smile, there's a weight you carry in silence—
the kind of burden that doesn't show up in family photos
or casual conversations.

It's the silent ache that lingers behind the small talk,
the invisible heaviness you've learned to carry,
even when your heart feels too shattered to piece back together.

A quiet endurance that holds back the tears
while still showing up for the world around you.

Grief Changed Me—So Did Grace

It made me ache in ways I didn't know were possible.

If they couldn't hear me when I was crying out for help,
how could they possibly hear me in the silence of my darkest moments?

When my voice felt too small, too broken to carry the weight of my
grief.
When every whispered plea felt like it was swallowed by the empty air,
lost in the quiet echoes of a house that no longer felt like home.

Grief is like a monster that lurks outside your home at night—
holding a flashlight,
shining it directly into your soul,
waiting to haunt you when you least expect it.

That monster isn't kind.
It wants to rob you of everything—
every joy,
every kindness,
every bit of happiness you've worked so hard to rebuild.

You can try to run,
but it always catches up.

Grief Changed Me—So Did Grace

They didn't say it out loud,
but their eyes said it all:
'She isn't over her loss yet,'
'She fell apart,'
'She's losing her mind,'
'She will never be the same again,'
'It's time for her to move on.'

Most people don't realize the weight grief leaves behind—
until it's theirs to carry.
It's easy to judge what you've never had to live through.

The sad truth is…
we're all broken in some way.
None of us chose to be strong.
We had to be strong.

The world doesn't know what to do with a person who has come
completely undone.
Some friendships quietly slip away—
even the ones you and your spouse once shared daily.

They praise your resilience.
Clap at your strength.
Say you've handled everything with grace,
when you hold everything together in public.

Grief Changed Me—So Did Grace

Never noticing the quiet unraveling that happens when you're alone—
when the world you once trusted feels impossibly distant.

So I kept going.
Kept rebuilding our life.
Through the tears,
through the graduations,
through all the cheer practices and comps,
school programs, and work events.

I smiled at everyone passing by me.
Kindly said that we're "doing okay" when people asked.
Just hoping that someone would notice
that I was ready to crumble at any given moment.

Most don't mean to fade away,
but they do.

And suddenly, you're left grieving more than your husband—
you're grieving the silence where connection used to be.

Grief Changed Me—So Did Grace

It's one of many heartbreaks no one warns you about.
And that's when you learn—
nobody around you can see the pain when you're smiling.

There were nights I lay in bed,
screaming into my pillow—
my cries muffled but full of meaning.
Begging—just begging—for relief from the pain.

Then, in the stillness of the silence,
I heard a voice—not loud, but steady.
Almost like it was God Himself,
whispering just for me to hear:

You must feel this pain to heal.
It's the echo of the love you shared,
the bond you still carry.
I know it hurts.
I feel your loss.
I feel your heart breaking—but I am still with you.
But you must pull yourself up.
No one else is coming to save you.

You are the miracle walking this earth.
You are the angel who will help others rise and ascend.
You are one of many lights.
And your light—will lead others out of the darkness.

Grief Changed Me—So Did Grace

Feeling and sitting with the weight of the pain—
that's crushing you like a ten-ton weight—
takes so much mental strength,
courage,
and bravery.

I feared moving forward,
because I didn't want to feel any more pain.
The more I moved forward,
the more I felt like I was moving further away from my loved one.

My kids needed me as much as I needed them.
I had to do it for them,
even if I couldn't do it for myself in that part of my journey.

And my kids became my why, every day.
Every single day, I lived for my kids.

I refused to let the weight of grief consume me—
not when they still needed my strength.

Grief Changed Me—So Did Grace

It became my mission to make sure my kids could see the best in
everything,
no matter what life throws at them.

I wanted to be their example—
that even in the hardest times,
you can gather every broken piece
and begin again.

From scratch.
From sorrow.
And still build something beautiful—
a beautiful life.

But even behind the smile,
there is strength—
a quiet, unbreakable resolve
that refuses to be silenced,
even in the heaviest moments.

Because behind every forced grin,
behind every whispered, "I'm okay,"
there is a heart still learning to carry its own weight,
still finding ways to keep going,
even when the world feels impossibly heavy.

Grief Changed Me—So Did Grace

As she began to rebuild,
she realized her strength wasn't just in pushing through the pain,
but in allowing herself to keep loving,
keep remembering,
and keep moving forward—
no matter how heavy the weight felt.

She didn't want her grief to steal the softness she once carried—
the gentle, open-hearted way she loved before everything changed.

And slowly, moment by moment,
her smile began to bloom again—
this time, not out of duty,
but out of healing.

Even behind the smile,
the love never left.
It just needed a place to be.

Grief Changed Me—So Did Grace

And if you find yourself in the darkness,
wondering if you'll ever feel whole again,
remember this:

The strength you've built in your hardest moments isn't just survival—
it's a quiet, steady resilience.
You have kept moving,
kept loving,
and kept hoping,
even when the weight felt impossible.

You are learning to live again,
to breathe again,
to love again.

You are not just what you've endured—
you are finding your way back to yourself.

Grief Changed Me—So Did Grace

As she found her way back to herself,
she realized that part of healing
was letting his spirit remain a part of her everyday life—
not just in memories,
but in the way she continued to live,
speak,
and love without apology.

She learned to speak about him—
not in hushed tones,
but with full, open love in her voice.

To say his name without hesitation,
not to make others uncomfortable,
but to keep his presence alive.

She needed to talk about him—
that was one of many things keeping her moving forward.

It takes courage to carry the weight of grief
while still holding onto the softness you once knew.
To speak their name without fear,
to let their memory live in the light,
and to keep moving forward
even when the weight feels unbearable.

Grief Changed Me—So Did Grace

Then come the milestones—
those firsts that feel like cruel reminders
that time keeps moving,
even though your world has stopped

Their birthday.
Your anniversary.
The holidays.
Even the changing seasons.

Each one arrives like a wave you didn't see coming,
knocking the wind out of you.

So she lit candles.
She ordered his favorite cake.
Some years, she yelled his name proudly.
Other times, she just sat in the quiet and cried.
And—yes—she had a beer for him,
the kind he always reached for after a long day.

Some days, that's how I honored him.
Other days, I just curled up and survived it.

There's no guidebook for how to handle the days
that once held love and laughter—
the days that now ache with absence.

And every one of those firsts becomes a thread
that ties your heart to theirs in a new way.

There's no right way to honor the person you lost.
Even if all you do is survive it—
that's still a form of remembering.

Grief Changed Me—So Did Grace

What used to be shared
becomes something you carry alone.

And no matter how you choose to show up,
it's okay.

Because just surviving those firsts
is a form of strength no one sees.

To smile at the memories
and let them live alongside the ache.

Love didn't leave.
It just changed form.

I wish someone had warned me
how hard it would be to shift from 'us,' 'we,' and 'ours'
to 'my,' 'me,' and 'mine.'

But in time, you learn to carry both—
the love that remains,
and the life that continues.
You learn to hold space for what was lost,
without losing yourself in the echoes.
You learn to stand,
even in the emptiest rooms.

That change alone was a heartbreak of its own.

Grief Changed Me—So Did Grace

And this is how I've learned to honor them—
not just in grief,
but in the way I continue to live and love.

To carry their love,
values,
hopes,
and dreams forward.

They are not just a memory.
They are a guiding force.

We built a beautiful life together.
We created a beautiful family.
And no matter what,
we will always be a beautiful family.
We will always have that to carry with us.

Those memories helped me survive,
through some of the damaging times in life.

That is what gives me the strength to keep moving,
to keep choosing life,
even in the face of loss.

Because the love we built didn't end.
It just shifted—
from something I held with them,
to something I carry within me.
And that is a strength that cannot be taken—
a quiet, enduring reminder
that love, once shared, never truly leaves.

Grief Changed Me—So Did Grace

We found several ways to cope as we strived to move forward.

At night, when the sun went down and our home fell silent,
we'd turn on our favorite songs
and have dance-off nights in the kitchen.

These weren't just distractions.
They were tiny rebellions against the weight of grief—
moments when we chose to live,
to laugh,
to let our bodies find their rhythm again.

The world outside didn't matter in those moments.
It was just us, dancing through the pain,
letting our hearts beat a little louder.

We had to keep moving forward—
even if it was just through a silly kitchen dance party
or a made-up game that made us laugh for five seconds longer.

Because in those fleeting moments of laughter,
we found a little light in the darkness,
a reminder that even in the heaviest seasons,
joy can still break through.

Grief Changed Me—So Did Grace

And somewhere along the way,
I realized something important:
I didn't have to let go of you to move forward.

I could carry you with me—
your love,
your lessons,
your memory.

Maybe that's the secret to healing—
not letting go,
but remembering in a way that finally brings peace.

We didn't stop being a family.
We just became a different kind.

One that stands,
even when it feels like we've been broken a thousand times.

One that endures,
finding hard-won moments of peace.

One that moves forward,
even when the weight feels impossible.

And in carrying you forward,
I found the quiet strength to stand again.

Grief Changed Me—So Did Grace

— "Grief is just love with no place to go." — Jamie Anderson

Grief Changed Me—So Did Grace

Journaling Your Thoughts

Have you ever smiled to hide your pain?
What was going on beneath that smile?

Grief Changed Me—So Did Grace

Journaling Your Thoughts

What would you say to yourself in those moments
If you could go back with the wisdom you have now?

Grief Changed Me—So Did Grace

Uplifting Strength
by RoseAnn V. Shawiak

A lesser-known gem, this poem reflects on finding peace and strength amidst life's challenges:

Feeling an uplifting strength touching my soul,
Waking it from a long and difficult pastime
Of living alone in the interior of my being.

It's a gentle reminder of the quiet resilience we can find within ourselves.

Grief Changed Me—So Did Grace

3 THE STRENGTH TO RISE

Grief changes you.
It challenges the very core of who you are—
reframes your world in harsh, unrelenting ways.

When you're stuck inside the frame,
surrounded by pain,
it's hard to recognize the quiet strength
still holding you together.

Even in moments when it feels
like you're battling the entire world,
remember this—
your strength is far greater than the pain.

Grief Changed Me—So Did Grace

You might not feel it yet—
but it's there,
tucked deep inside you,
quietly waiting for the moment you're ready to rise.

You have so much tenacity,
strength,
and resilience within you.

I know this is one of the toughest battles
any of us have ever had to fight.
And there have been many battles along the way.

You will overcome this battle—
just like you've overcome every battle
life has thrown at you before.

Grief Changed Me—So Did Grace

But here's something I wish someone had told me from the beginning:

Healing isn't something you cross off a list—
it curves,
it pauses,
it circles back.

There's more than one stage of healing.
And you don't just go from "hurt" to "healed."
You can feel every stage of healing all at once.
You don't have to reject one just to embrace another.

Sometimes, you won't even know which stage you're in
until you're deep in it.

And that's normal.

You've experienced something so tragic,
so heartbreaking,
and yet here you are, still moving.

The pain doesn't mean you're broken—
it means you're learning how to live with all the parts of you.
The balance is learning how to walk with all stages of grief.

Grief Changed Me—So Did Grace

Every version of you that shows up along the way—
the broken,
the angry,
the lost,
and even the whole—
has something to teach you.

Don't rush through any of them.
They're all part of your becoming.

The hard versions will teach you resilience.
The tender ones will teach you compassion.

You will learn to stop resisting the new versions of yourself and start
nurturing who you're becoming.

You'll start loving yourself,
appreciating all the ways you've forever changed.

And together,
they will lead you to the most beautiful version of who you truly are.

Grief Changed Me—So Did Grace

In those early days, it felt like I was only surviving—
holding on with both hands to a life I no longer recognized.

But over time, I discovered that true strength isn't just surviving—it's
learning to rise.

I didn't know anything beyond putting one foot in front of the other—
just forcing myself to get through the day without falling apart.

I was doing everything I could to show up for my kids,
to try to hold onto what we had left of our life from the ashes,
even as my heart felt shattered.

The world kept spinning,
but I felt frozen in place—
tethered to a pain that refused to let go.

But slowly, like a tree growing around a wound,
I began to rise.

Grief Changed Me—So Did Grace

People won't always show up the way you hoped they would.
Some disappear.
Some surprise you.
But it rarely goes the way you once believed it might.

You'll begin to find strength in the smallest acts—
making it through a day without crying,
laughing with your kids,
choosing not to answer the phone.

Healing doesn't happen in giant leaps.
It comes in hesitant, unsteady inches—
each one earned through tears,
silence,
and quiet courage.

Steps no one sees.

Grief Changed Me—So Did Grace

Even as I struggled through the weight of trauma,
I found that every small act of moving forward
was a quiet act of courage—
each one a reminder that I was still here.

Grief Changed Me—So Did Grace

I struggled with PTSD—
haunted by a thousand reminders.

Signing papers felt like lifting the shattered pieces
of a life I could barely hold.

Every call,
every question,
every thought,
every decision,
every uncertain step felt like navigating a minefield.

I'd wake up in the middle of the night,
heart racing,
reaching for my children—
just to be sure they were still there,
still safe.

Certain words, even whispers,
could turn my whole day upside down—
shattering what little peace I'd managed to find.

Every decision felt like a weight only I could carry—
a constant reminder of the life I never imagined facing alone.

And every one of those moments
became a harsh reminder of how far I still had to go.

Grief Changed Me—So Did Grace

I didn't choose to hold on to my grief—
it simply became part of me,
familiar and strangely comforting,
even as it weighed me down.

I had to slowly learn it was okay to let go of survival mode—
to make space for the person I was becoming.

I was healing, yes—
but still walking through the aftershocks of trauma,
especially the parts I couldn't control.

Grief Changed Me—So Did Grace

You'll forge yourself in the darkest moments—
the kind so disorienting,
you don't know if you're coming or going.

I know how hard it is to believe the sky is still blue
when darkness settles over you like a familiar blanket.

Change is terrifying—
especially when your whole world has already burned to ash,
and you're left standing in the smoke.
Unable to breathe.

Grief Changed Me—So Did Grace

I didn't want to hide behind a smile that only served others.
I wanted it to be real—
to mean something again.

You learn to stand tall,
to keep moving forward—
even when you're crying,
even when the darkest thoughts are stuck on repeat in your mind.

You can still stand tall
while feeling every emotion.

I kept my guard up.
I built a wall so high,
no one could climb it—
but deep down,
I was more than ready to lay down my sword.

I feared the unknown.
But truthfully,
we all live every day in the unknown.

When you get comfortable,
you start making excuses to stay stuck.

The moment I realized that scared me…
that was the same moment I knew
I had to push forward—
with every ounce of hope and grace I had left inside me.

Grief Changed Me—So Did Grace

Keep going.
When it's messy.
When you're scared.
When you're exhausted.
When every part of you wants to give up.

I know you're tired.
I know you feel broken.
But rest when you need to,
and rise when you can.

You're not alone,
and you're not finished.
This isn't the end of your story.

This is where you show yourself the most grace.

You don't have to know how to keep going.
Just know you're not alone.

Grief Changed Me—So Did Grace

I'm for you—
your biggest cheerleader.
Keep holding on,
even on your worst days.

Remain hopeful.
Remain faithful.
Remain humble.

You're still here.
Not because it's easy,
but because you've chosen to rise,
over and over again.

And that is a quiet kind of strength
the world rarely sees,
but always needs.

Grief Changed Me—So Did Grace

Most of all—trust yourself.
You already have everything you need to make it through the worst
storms of your life.

You gather every shattered piece of your broken heart
and begin gluing them back together—
not with invisible thread,
but with golden seams—
the kind that hold not just your pain,
but every hard-earned piece of your resilience.

The kind that turns every wound into something sacred.

You'll realize:
you can rebuild—from the ashes, from the ache,
from all that you've endured—
and still create something beautiful ahead.

Grief Changed Me—So Did Grace

As I rebuilt,
I realized I didn't want the fast-paced life I once had.

I wanted something slower, a quiet life,
one more peaceful.

I wanted to wake up to the sound of birds,
to drink my coffee slowly watching the sunrise spill across my porch,
to feel the earth in my hands as I tended a garden surrounded by the
beauty of nature.

I remember one morning,
sitting on my porch with a warm cup of coffee in my hands,
when a red cardinal landed on the arm of a nearby chair.

For a moment, everything felt still.
It was a gentle reminder that life goes on,
even in the quiet,
even in the grief.

It's not weakness to choose quiet over noise,
stillness over rushing.

It's a brave choice to listen to your heart,
to let it catch up with your body,
to find peace in the spaces where chaos used to live.

It's a kind of strength all its own—
a strength that comes from honoring the ache,
from letting the quiet become a place of comfort,
and from remembering that sometimes the softest moments can carry
you the furthest.

Grief Changed Me—So Did Grace

I craved a life that made me feel like the woman I had fought so hard
to become.
Alive. Present. Whole.
Not just busy.

I wanted to notice the small things—
the way the sun gently kissed my face,
the sound of the wind moving through the trees,
the simple comfort of bare feet in the grass.

But for months, I kept trying to move at the pace we once lived—
a life that no longer fit.
The life he and I had shared.
Isn't that what healing meant?
Getting back to normal?

I rushed through my grief, thinking that if I healed fast enough,
I could rejoin the world that hadn't stopped when mine fell apart.

But the truth is,
rushing only delayed my healing.
I put bandages on wounds that needed real tending—
and called it progress.

It kept me from truly understanding what I needed. I longed for soft
days and quiet routines—
a life that didn't demand I rush through what was sacred.

I wasn't just trying to find a way forward—
I was learning to honor both the life I lost
and the person I was becoming.

I needed the kind of life that felt real,
where I could find space for both the grief and the growth.

Grief Changed Me—So Did Grace

I realized that peace didn't just mean quiet.
It meant choosing to embrace the stillness,
to let my heart breathe,
to make room for both the ache and the healing.

It meant letting the quiet become a place of comfort,
not just a reminder of what I had lost,
but a space to find strength in the stillness.

Grief Changed Me—So Did Grace

Grief didn't just change me—
it stripped away the noise,
the rush,
the endless list of things that once felt important.

Then something shifted.
A craving I couldn't name at the time, but I understand now:
Grief changed my values.
My desires. My pace.

You don't have to perform. You don't have to prove. You can just be.

It forced me to pause,
to listen,
to redefine what truly mattered.

It reminded me that a full life isn't measured by busyness or noise,
but by the quiet moments that makes your heart feel whole again.

It taught me that real strength isn't just in surviving the chaos,
but in finding peace when the world feels heavy.

It taught me that a meaningful life isn't just about pushing through,
but about finding moments of stillness that let you breathe and truly
live.

Grief Changed Me—So Did Grace

I needed to be still.
A life that allowed space for me to heal-
not just survive.

I've learned that there's strength in slowing down,
in choosing peace over chaos,
in letting your mind catch up with the life you're building.

A softer kind of strength—
the kind born in the pauses between the pain,
that honors the quiet spaces,
can carry you farther than you ever imagined.

It's a strength that whispers,
even in the silence,
that you are still here—
growing, mending,
finding your way back to yourself,
and rising from the ashes
with a heart that has learned to find its own steady beat again.

Grief Changed Me—So Did Grace

Grief didn't end your story.
It simply changed the way you carry it.

You carry them forward—
in every breath,
every choice,
every quiet act of courage.

And maybe the greatest miracle of all—
is that you're still becoming, even now.

Not in spite of the loss.
But because the love never left—
it just found a new way to stay.

You carry them forward with you.
Not in the way you once imagined,
but in a way that honors them
and honors the person you are becoming.

And in that honoring,
you will find your strength to rise.

Not because the storm ended,
but because you chose to.

You are not just what you've lost.
You are what you choose to carry forward.

The memories,
the love,
the lessons—
each piece a testament to your resilience.

Grief Changed Me—So Did Grace

You are forever growing, evolving.
And that is something beautiful.

Grief Changed Me—So Did Grace

— "You may not control all the events that happen to you, but you can decide not to be reduced by them." — Maya Angelou

Grief Changed Me—So Did Grace

Journaling your Thoughts

What was one time you surprised yourself with your strength—even if it didn't feel like strength at the time?

Grief Changed Me—So Did Grace

Journaling your Thoughts

What was one time you surprised yourself with your strength—even if it didn't feel like strength at the time?

Grief Changed Me—So Did Grace

4 THE MANY FACES OF HEALING

Grief hits like a wave—
sudden, overwhelming,
and impossible to prepare for.

One moment you're okay,
the next you're gasping for air.

You might be questioning everything—
wondering if God, the universe,
or fate made some kind of terrible mistake
by taking them away from you.

As healing begins—
quietly, slowly—
you'll meet unfamiliar versions of yourself.

Grief Changed Me—So Did Grace

Some broken.
Some brave.
Some stronger.
Some you won't even recognize.

Each version of you holds pieces of who you were—
and every one of them brings you closer to who you're becoming.

Grief Changed Me—So Did Grace

This journey isn't about returning to who you once were—
because that version of you no longer exists.

It's about discovering who you are now,
in the sacred space that loss has left behind.

After losing everything,
I found myself wandering through rooms in our new house—
each step echoing with a silence that was too loud,
too empty.

The home that once held laughter and shared moments
now stood still—
quiet witnesses to a grief that had settled into every corner.

Every room felt foreign,
like I was walking through someone else's life.

Grief Changed Me—So Did Grace

Even beneath the heavy weight of grief,
there are moments of peace—
brief, unexpected,
and quietly powerful.

Some days,
a ray of sunlight breaks through the clouds,
warming your skin and reminding you
that comfort still exists.

Sometimes it's the smell of rain,
or rabbits playing in your garden,
squirrels playing in the trees—
subtle reminders that beauty hasn't disappeared from the world.

These small, quiet moments become sacred gifts on the journey
through grief.

They don't erase the sadness,
but they remind you that healing doesn't grow only from pain—
it also rises slowly through these moments of quiet grace,
piece by piece,
becoming something new.

Grief Changed Me—So Did Grace

There were countless days
when it felt like a victory just to make it to the sofa—
overwhelmed by the crushing weight of grief.

The silence was deafening.

In those quiet moments,
I searched for something—anything—
that might remind me I wasn't entirely alone.

It wasn't always obvious,
but sometimes there were signs—
tiny flickers of hope that slipped through the cracks of my broken
heart,
like distant stars breaking through the darkness.

A cloud shaped like a heart.
A reminder that love hadn't left—
only changed form.

Happiness and sadness can coexist.
Cherish every moment when it comes.

Grief Changed Me—So Did Grace

Some days I didn't recognize myself.
Other days, I saw someone stronger than before.

I knew I wasn't perfect.
I'd made mistakes—because I'm human, just like you.

I've suffered, like so many others in this world.
I've felt deep, unimaginable loss.

Every one of us has a story.
And that's why I had to tell mine.

I realized healing wasn't about returning—
it was about re-creating.

Not who I used to be,
but who I was meant to become now.

Grief Changed Me—So Did Grace

Survivor's guilt is its own stage of grief.

I felt guilty for living—
for being the one still here,
still breathing,
still watching my children grow.

It crept into my thoughts,
shadowed every moment of joy,
and turned even the simplest pleasures
into quiet reminders of all that had been lost.

It waited for me in every laugh,
every hug,
every purchase,
every family event.

And perhaps this is why the 'firsts' after loss can feel so isolating—
because every new experience is marked by their absence,
every celebration a reminder that they should still be here.

Grief Changed Me—So Did Grace

Guilt was woven into every corner of my life.
I couldn't escape it.

It was there in the echoes of our lost routines,
in the empty space beside me,
in the moments I felt I should still be doing something for him.

Even the smallest decisions felt heavy,
as if every choice I made without him
was a betrayal of the life we once shared.

It lingered in every breath I took without him,
in every sunrise I witnessed alone,
in every quiet moment I found myself still here,
while he was not.

Grief hides in the ordinary.

Even a simple salt and pepper shaker
can carry the weight of everything you've lost.

Grief Changed Me—So Did Grace

I started apologizing for everything and everyone—
sometimes for things I hadn't done,
for misunderstandings that only existed in my mind,
for the fear that I had somehow let everyone down
without even realizing it.

I moved through my days braced for the next wave of pain,
always half-expecting another loss,
another heartbreak,
another disappointment,
as if the chaos had become my only certainty.

Grief Changed Me—So Did Grace

The 'firsts' after loss are like waves you didn't see coming—
knocking the wind out of you,
forcing you to find your footing
in a world forever changed.

They are markers not just of absence,
but of survival—
quiet steps toward learning to live again,
even when the weight feels impossible.

Grief Changed Me—So Did Grace

Their birthday.
Your anniversary.
The holidays.
Even the changing of the seasons.

Grief Changed Me—So Did Grace

Each one finds its way through the cracks in the walls you've tried to
rebuild—
an ache that catches you off guard,
a reminder of all that has changed.

You want to honor them,
to celebrate their life,
but you're not always sure how.

Do you bake their favorite cake?
Light a candle?
Say their name out loud?
Have a beer for them?
Or do you just curl up and survive it?

Grief Changed Me—So Did Grace

There's no guidebook for how to face the days that once held joy.

Now, they ache with absence.

What used to be shared
becomes something you carry alone.

And however you choose to show up—
it's okay.

Because just surviving those "firsts"
is a quiet kind of strength no one sees.

Grief Changed Me—So Did Grace

In that first year,
I found myself trying to keep our life running
as if he were still here—
making every decision
as though he were sitting beside me.

But then the second year arrived—
a year when the weight of reality truly settles in.

It's the year when you start to accept what you've been through.

I noticed myself making decisions without considering what he would
have wanted—
not because I loved him any less,
but because I was beginning to accept
that he wasn't coming back.

That I would have to build my life , my kids life, going forward,
carrying his memory but not waiting for his return.

It wasn't until I began to accept this new, unwanted reality—
and slowly made peace with it—
that I could breathe again.

Grief Changed Me—So Did Grace

That's when I started to feel something like closure.
A quiet knowing that my person wouldn't want me to carry guilt,
grief,
sadness,
and pain forever.

They would want me to live—
live because of them,
and for them.

Grief Changed Me—So Did Grace

I stopped apologizing for my grief.
I let the tears fall freely,
allowed the silence to speak,
and finally made peace with the chaos.

This was healing—
not clean,
not quick,
not easy—
but real.

Grief Changed Me—So Did Grace

Healing wasn't about returning to who I used to be.
It was about learning to honor the woman I was becoming—
one day at a time.

Grief Changed Me—So Did Grace

You'll learn to walk with both the darkness and the light.

Some days, the darkness will feel overwhelming—
like it could swallow you whole.

But there will also be moments when the light breaks through—
even if it's just for a second.
And that's enough.

Grief Changed Me—So Did Grace

You'll learn to carry both the weight of your grief
and the light of your hope.

And in doing so,
you'll grow stronger,
more whole,
and gain a deeper understanding of yourself
and the life you're slowly rebuilding.

Grief Changed Me—So Did Grace

It's already within you—
everything you need is inside you.

In your darkest moments,
you'll find a brave strength still alive within you—
a small but unshakable part of you
that refuses to be lost,
even when the world feels heavy.

Grief Changed Me—So Did Grace

Embrace it.
Welcome it with open arms.

Know this:
you are worthy of building a new foundation—
one that walks alongside your grief,
not beneath it.

Grief Changed Me—So Did Grace

You are the keeper of your own healing.

The one piecing together a life you never planned for,
slowly learning to call it your own.

Grief Changed Me—So Did Grace

You deserve a life where hope,
peace,
and love are not just possibilities,
but promises.

Grief Changed Me—So Did Grace

Start planting seeds today.
Let hope take root.

And one day,
your new life will bloom—
right where sorrow once lived.

Grief Changed Me—So Did Grace

— "Healing isn't about changing who you are; it's about discovering who you've always been." — Unknown

Grief Changed Me—So Did Grace

Journaling your Thoughts

What would you say to yourself in those moments if you could go back with the wisdom, you have now?

Grief Changed Me—So Did Grace

Journaling your Thoughts

How has your grief changed over time? What emotions or phases have surfaced along the way?

Grief Changed Me—So Did Grace

Journaling your Thoughts

What does healing look like to you now? Has your definition of healing shifted since the beginning of your journey?

Grief Changed Me—So Did Grace

5 CARRYING THE LOVE FORWARD

We refuse to be defined by others.
Their thoughts and opinions no longer matter—
because they no longer serve us on this journey.

We are moving forward.
Toward happiness.
Peace.
Toward a life that feels a little lighter.
And new memories—
ones forged in the fire that tried to destroy us.

Grief Changed Me—So Did Grace

We've endured heartbreak so deep,
loss so devastating…
and yet here we are.
Still standing.
Still moving.

Grief Changed Me—So Did Grace

We are not just survivors.
We are the quiet, unbreakable souls
who choose to live again.
To rebuild a life from the shattered pieces.
To find purpose in the chaos.
To reach for the light,
even when the weight of grief clings to your every step.

Because in the darkness,
we are still searching for the fragments of ourselves—
still choosing to show up,
still finding ways to love through the loss.

Grief Changed Me—So Did Grace

We are the ones who keep going—
not because it's easy,
but because it's necessary.

Because our lives, though changed, still have meaning.
Because the love we carry forward demands it.
Because there are still small, quiet moments of joy
waiting to be discovered,
even in the shadow of loss.

We keep going because, in our hearts,
we know that survival is a tribute—
to the love we lost,
to the people we've become,
and to the lives we're still meant to live.

Grief Changed Me—So Did Grace

The love you carry for them hasn't vanished—
it's transformed.

It's no longer a constant weight.
It's a guiding force—
leading you through the darkest of days.

It's in the way I reach for strength
I never knew I had.
In the way I still whisper their name
when the house falls silent.
In the way my children carry their values,
their kindness,
their laughter.

That love didn't vanish.
It lives in the spaces they once filled,
in the habits and rituals they left behind,
and in the quiet, everyday moments
where their memory lingers.

Grief Changed Me—So Did Grace

Those memories kept me breathing—
through the hardest, most soul-crushing moments.

I found myself clinging to small routines,
quiet rituals that pulled me back from the edge.

It wasn't always the grand gestures that saved me.
Sometimes, it was the gentle act of holding my children a little longer,
their small, steady breaths reminding me
that there was still life around me,
still love to be felt.

Grief Changed Me—So Did Grace

It was the way my fingers would trace the pages he once wrote in his
notebook,
running over the same words he once lingered on,
trying to hold onto the pieces of him that still lived once.

The way my children's laughter would echo through our new house,
their voices a living reminder of his presence,
proof that his spirit lives on through them—
that the best parts of him still exist,
woven into the fabric of their lives.

And the way I'd pause when his favorite song came on the radio,
letting the ache rise and fall like a slow, familiar tide,
allowing the memories to wash over me,
settling into my bones,
reminding me that even in the quiet, broken pieces of my life,
there was still a pulse—
still a reason to keep going,
still a thread connecting me to the life I had loved so deeply.

Grief Changed Me—So Did Grace

A reminder that even in the thick of grief,
there is still room for joy,
for laughter,
for love to break through the cracks.

Those moments became our way of saying,
"We are still here."
And that was enough.

Grief Changed Me—So Did Grace

On the hardest days,
I searched for distractions.
Anything to fill the endless hours.
Anything to shield my kids from the full weight of my grief.

We watched funny movies that used to bring us joy—
pretending, for a moment, that everything was okay.

But even in those bursts of laughter,
the ache remained.

A quiet reminder that the darkness was still close by.
Grief and love became intertwined—
two sides of the same coin.

Every laugh felt like a rebellion against the sadness.
Every small dance a defiance against the emptiness.

But those moments taught me something—
that even in the quiet of shadows,
the heart remembers how to beat.
Even in the depths of loss,
the soul longs for peace.

Grief Changed Me—So Did Grace

I made a quiet vow to myself:
When I reached the other side of the darkness,
I would choose the light—
deliberately and without apology.

Not every day felt like a victory,
but I began to see that even the smallest moments of hope
could lead to change.

I promised myself that no matter how heavy the past felt,
I would keep moving toward peace—
and begin to accept everything I had endured.

Grief Changed Me—So Did Grace

I didn't just carry the loss.
I carried the love.
The memories.
The lessons.

I carried the warmth of his smile,
the echo of his heartbeat,
and the unspoken promises we made to keep living.

I carried the strength to rise again,
even when my heart felt too heavy to carry itself.

I realized that moving forward didn't mean leaving him behind.
It meant carrying him with me—
through every sunset,
every whispered prayer,
every quiet act of courage.

Grief Changed Me—So Did Grace

I found him in the smallest things—
the way light spilled across the kitchen counter,
revealing a heart etched in stone.

The familiar tune of a song we once danced to.
The way our children laughed—
just like he did.

Even the way his truck looks in the garage.

These moments became sacred—
stitched into my new life.
Not as replacements,
but as reminders that love doesn't just disappear.

It changes form,
weaving itself into the quiet corners of our days.

Grief Changed Me—So Did Grace

I learned to speak about him—
not in hushed tones,
but with open love in my voice.

I said his name,
not to make others uncomfortable,
but to keep him alive.

Because in saying his name,
I kept his presence close—
I kept his laughter in our home,
I kept his love in my heart,
and I kept his spirit alive
in the way I continued to choose life,
even when it felt impossible.

Talking about him was one of the things that kept me moving forward.

Because saying his name
meant refusing to let the silence erase him.

Grief Changed Me—So Did Grace

The milestones—
those beautiful, gentle reminders
that grow lighter over time,
becoming memories you can smile through
without breaking down.

You remember their smile on their birthday.
Your favorite anniversary song.
The holidays full of laughter.
Their favorite traditions.

Each one holding pieces of the life you shared.

Grief Changed Me—So Did Grace

I lit candles.
I ordered his favorite cake.
Some days, I talked about him nonstop.
Other days, I sat in the quiet and cried.

And yes—
I had a beer or two for him.
The kind he always reached for after a long day.

In those moments,
that's how I chose to honor him—
not just by remembering the loss,
but by celebrating the love that still lives on in those memories.

Grief Changed Me—So Did Grace

With time, these milestones begin to take on new meaning.
What once felt like a wound becomes a marker of survival.
They are reminders of the life you shared
and the strength it takes to keep moving forward.

These days don't just pass—
they shape you.

They remind you of the person you've become,
of the love you continue to carry,
and of the quiet, unbreakable courage
that never lets you stay in the dark for too long.

Grief Changed Me—So Did Grace

But survival isn't just about enduring the storm.

It's about finding the quiet, sacred reminders
that keep you moving forward.

It's the way a children hugs you
at the end of a long day.

It's the way light reflects
in the empty corners of memory,
touching the spaces where his presence still lingers,
even after all that's been lost.

It's the slow, steady rhythm of a heart
that dared to keep beating,
even when it felt like it had shattered.

Grief Changed Me—So Did Grace

Grief can be relentless,
but so is love.

And where love lingers,
hope finds its way back.

It might not be the kind of hope you once knew,
but it's there—
patient and graceful,
waiting for you to notice it.

It's the warmth of a familiar touch.
The first time you catch yourself smiling without hesitation.
The way a song that once felt too heavy
now carries a softness in your heart.

Grief Changed Me—So Did Grace

It's finding the courage to make new plans,
to welcome new people into your life,
and to let love grow in places once marked by sorrow.

In those moments,
you realize that healing isn't just one leaf on a tree during summer.

It's the entire cycle—
the falling,
the withering,
the quiet gathering of strength before the bloom.

A slow, steady return to the parts of yourself
you thought were lost.

The gentle acceptance
that even broken branches can hold nests again.

That a heart cracked by loss
can still be a sanctuary for love.

Learning that, like the trees,
you can grow around your wounds,
finding new strength in the very places you once felt hollow.

Grief Changed Me—So Did Grace

It's the way you keep reaching for the light,
even when shadows linger.

The patient act of allowing yourself
to come back to life,
over and over,
in small, quiet ways.

Like a forest recovers after a fire—
slowly,
almost imperceptibly,
as green shoots break through the ash.

The quiet resilience of roots
that hold on
even when the world above seems stripped bare.

The gentle unfurling of a leaf
that chooses to reach for the sun again,
even after the harshest of winters.

Grief Changed Me—So Did Grace

Healing isn't a destination—
it's a return to life.

It's the slow rebuilding of a heart
that has weathered countless storms
and yet still chooses to beat.

It's the small, sacred act of becoming whole again,
piece by fragile piece.

Grief Changed Me—So Did Grace

In the way you carve out small moments of hope each day.
In the way you come back to yourself,
again and again,
in small, uncelebrated ways.

Like the way a river carves a path through stone—
persistent, steady, and unyielding,
even when the journey seems impossible.

Or the way wildflowers push through cracked pavement,
unseen, uncelebrated,
finding life in the harshest conditions.

The quiet endurance of mountains—
unchanged by passing storms,
standing firm as the world shifts around them,
their strength found not in resistance,
but in the unwavering certainty of their foundation.

And in the way you've learned to stand again,
even when the ground beneath you feels unsteady.
To rise from the ashes of a life forever changed.
To find a way forward,
even as you carry the weight of all you've lost.
To grow through the cracks,
and hold firm through the storms—
proof that even in the rubble,
there is still strength,
still life,
still the quiet, steady pulse of a heart wanting to live again.

Grief Changed Me—So Did Grace

Because even in the midst of grief,
there is still life to be lived.
There are still moments worth holding,
still steps worth taking,
still reasons to keep going.

Grief Changed Me—So Did Grace

There's no guidebook for how to face the days
that once held love and laughter—
the days that now ache with absence.

Every one of those firsts becomes a thread
that ties your heart to theirs in a new way.

There's no right way to honor the person you lost.
Even if all you do is survive it—
that's still a form of remembering.

What was once shared
becomes something you now carry alone.

And however you choose to show up—
it's okay.

Because just surviving those firsts
is a quiet kind of strength no one sees.

To smile at the memories...
and let them live beside the ache.

Love didn't leave.
It simply changed form.

Grief Changed Me—So Did Grace

After losing my spouse, I lost more than just a part of myself—
I lost the version of my children I had imagined,
the future I had hoped for,
and the family we were meant to be.

I watched my children's innocence shatter in the same moment my own
heart broke.
Their laughter, once so effortless, became guarded—
a fragile thing that might break under the weight of this new, unspoken
pain.
I saw their childhoods take on a different shape—
one where joy and grief shared the same small, sacred space.

As a mother, my instinct was to shield them,
to carry their grief alongside my own,
but there were days when I felt like I was failing them—
when my own sorrow felt too heavy to bear, let alone theirs.

I mourned not only the life we once had
but also the future I had envisioned for them—
the carefree years, the endless hugs from their dad,
the sound of his voice cheering them on at every milestone.

Grief Changed Me—So Did Grace

It's a quiet kind of heartbreak
to watch your children struggle to find their footing
in a world that feels forever changed—
to see their small shoulders carry a loss
they should never have known so young.

But as they learned to live without him, so did I.
Together, we created new memories
into our broken lives.
We found new ways to be a family,
even when the pieces didn't fit quite the same.

And though it felt impossible at times,
we learned to carry his love forward,
each in our own way—
proving that even in the depths of grief,
life can find a way to grow.

Grief Changed Me—So Did Grace

I wish someone had warned me
how hard it would be to shift from us,
we, and ours...
to my,
me,
and mine.

That change alone was a heartbreak of its own.

Grief Changed Me—So Did Grace

It's not just the empty chair at the table
or the quiet space beside you in bed.

The thousand little moments
that remind you of the life you once shared—
the inside jokes no one else remembers,
the unspoken understanding you once took for granted,
the way you could read each other without a single word.

Reaching for their opinion,
only to remember that the conversation now lives in your heart.

Silent decisions you make alone,
the ones you never imagined facing without them.

The quiet ache that settles in the depth of your soul
when you realize that the life you once built together
has become a solo journey.

Grief Changed Me—So Did Grace

But this—
this is how I honor them through my journey.

By carrying their love forward.
Their values.
Their hopes.
Their dreams.

We built a beautiful life together.
We created a beautiful family.

And no matter what,
we will always be a beautiful family.

That is something we will always carry.

Even as the years pass
and the seasons change,
their love still echoes in the quiet moments.

Grief Changed Me—So Did Grace

It's in the way I reach for strength
I never knew I had.

In the way I still whisper their name
when the house falls silent.

In the way my children carry their spirit,
their kindness,
their laughter.

That love didn't vanish.
It lives in the spaces they once filled,
in the habits and rituals they left behind,
and in the quiet, everyday moments
where their memory lingers.

Grief Changed Me—So Did Grace

Those memories helped me survive—
especially during the hardest,
most damaging years of life.

We found small ways to cope
as we tried to move forward.

At night,
when the sun went down and the house grew quiet,
we'd turn on our favorite songs
and have dance-offs in the kitchen.

The world outside didn't matter in those moments.

It was just us—
dancing through the pain,
letting our hearts beat a little louder.

We had to keep moving forward,
even if it was through a silly kitchen dance
or a made-up game that made us laugh
for just five seconds longer.

It was in those small, fleeting moments
that I felt something close to peace.

A reminder that even in the thick of grief,
there is still room for joy,
for laughter,
for love to break through the cracks.

Those moments became our way of saying,
"We are still here."

And that was enough.

Grief Changed Me—So Did Grace

We are still a family.
A different kind, perhaps.
But still a family.
And that is something we will always have.

Because love, once given, never truly leaves.
It lingers in the choices we make,
in the way we still gather for holidays,
in the way we keep living,
even when the world feels a little emptier.

Grief Changed Me—So Did Grace

As the years pass,
you learn to carry both the weight of grief
and the light of hope.

You become stronger,
not because the pain lessens,
but because you learn to live alongside it—
to carry it without letting it consume you.

You start to see the small, quiet miracles in your own survival.
You learn to breathe through the ache,
to dance through the heaviness,
to find grace in the chaos.

You discover that healing isn't about moving on—
it's about moving forward,
with all the love you've ever known still held close.

And in that quiet, sacred act,
you find your strength to rise again.

Grief Changed Me—So Did Grace

It's in the way you reach for a little more light each day.
The way you breathe through the ache.
The way you carry them in your heart,
even when the weight feels impossible to bear.

Grief Changed Me—So Did Grace

And as long as you remember,
that love remains a part of you—
woven into every breath,
every step,
every heartbeat.

They are still here.
Not just in memory,
but in the way you live.
In the love you continue to carry.

Grief Changed Me—So Did Grace

Somewhere along the way,
I realized something important:
I didn't have to let go of you to move forward.

I could carry you with me—
your love,
your lessons,
your memory.

Maybe that's the secret to healing.
Not letting go…
but remembering in a way that brings peace.

Grief Changed Me—So Did Grace

We didn't stop being a family.
We just became a different kind—
one shaped by small hands learning to hold on without him,
by the steady footsteps of children growing into their own strength.

A family built on the echoes of his laugh,
on the memories that fill our souls,
on the unspoken bond that still ties us together,
even as we find our footing in a world without him.

We learned to carry each other—
through the long nights,
through the small, quiet victories,
through the firsts without him,
and the milestones he will always be a part of.

A family that grew in ways we never expected—
learning to stand together,
even when the ground felt unsteady,
finding strength in each other,
even when it felt impossible.

And in carrying him forward,
I found the strength to carry myself, too.

Grief Changed Me—So Did Grace

Because even in the absence,
even in the quiet,
even in the shadowed corners of my heart,
you remain.

And as long as I keep moving,
as long as I keep breathing,
as long as I keep loving,
your light will never fade.

Grief Changed Me—So Did Grace

And that is enough.
That is everything.

That is a beautiful legacy—
one built on love that didn't end,
but found a new way to stay.

A legacy carried in the echoes of their laughter,
in the quiet strength they find in themselves,
in the way they carry his spirit forward,
woven into the fabric of their lives.

A legacy of quiet, unspoken strength—
the kind that rises from the ashes,
that dances in the kitchen,
that chooses to keep living,
even when the weight feels too heavy.

It's in the small, ordinary moments—
the bedtime stories,
the shared meals,
the whispered memories—
that his presence lingers.

It's in the way they carry his kindness,
his humor,
his fierce, unbreakable love.

Grief Changed Me—So Did Grace

And as long as they live,
so does he.

Because that is what love does.
It lives on,
even when the world feels broken.
It endures.
It carries us forward.

And that is a beautiful legacy.

Grief Changed Me—So Did Grace

— "Those we love never truly leave us. There are things that death cannot touch." — Jack Thorne

Grief Changed Me—So Did Grace

Journaling your Thoughts

In what ways do you carry the love of the person you lost with you today?

Grief Changed Me—So Did Grace

Journaling your Thoughts

What rituals, memories, or actions help you keep their presence alive in your daily life?

Grief Changed Me—So Did Grace

A Note on Forgiveness

Forgiveness is one of the quietest parts of grief—
and maybe one of the hardest.

I had to learn to forgive myself
for what I didn't know then.
For not being able to stop time.

I had to forgive others, too—
for their distance,
their silence,
their well-meant but painful words.

And maybe hardest of all,
I had to forgive life itself.

Not because it made sense.
But because carrying anger alongside grief
is too heavy for one heart to hold.

Grief Changed Me—So Did Grace

6 GRACE IN THE CHAOS

In the middle of the chaos,
she kept whispering one thing to herself:
choose grace.

Every day,
even when it felt impossible.
Even when the world felt heavy.

Because grace isn't a single choice—
it's a thousand small ones,
made quietly,
time and time again
until they become the thread that holds you steady.

Grief Changed Me—So Did Grace

Grace for the moments of rest—
the fleeting pauses when she allowed herself to breathe without guilt,
even if only for a second.

It wasn't easy.
But in giving herself grace,
she honored the journey,
the struggle,
and the quiet strength it took just to keep going.

Sometimes, the world demands too much— it asks you to smile
through the storm, to hold yourself together when you're unraveling, to
stay silent when your soul aches to scream.

But grace isn't just about quiet strength.
It's about knowing when to roar.

Grief Changed Me—So Did Grace

Trauma taught me to whisper—
to press my pain between clenched teeth,
to swallow the screams that burned my throat,
to stay silent for the sake of peace.

But peace never came.
Not for me.

For years, I mistook my silence for strength,
until I realized that true strength is found in speaking
even when your voice trembles.

Why was I holding my breath for others—
those who never gave me the safety to grieve,
who twisted my pain into their comfort,
who stayed at ease while I waged a silent war within myself?

No.
I'm done keeping the peace for those who never deserved it.
I won't stay quiet to make others comfortable.
I refuse to swallow my truth to spare their calm.

I'm finding my voice again,
letting it rise from the depths of my silenced spirit—
no longer whispering, but roaring.
I'm not just breaking the silence.
I'm reclaiming it.

Grief Changed Me—So Did Grace

Because grief doesn't always look like tears.
Sometimes, it's the silence that lingers
long after everyone else has gone.
The stillness in a room that once felt full.
The heaviness only she could feel.

She began walking away from the voices
that made her doubt everything—
her choices,
her worth,
even her right to heal.

Every step away from their shadows
is a step toward her own light—
toward the peace she fought to protect,
toward the truth she can no longer silence,
toward the woman she is becoming.

Grief Changed Me—So Did Grace

Choosing grace isn't just about survival.
It's about choosing yourself—
again and again,
no matter who tries to pull you back.

It took real strength to protect the fragile peace
she had finally found within.

In the chaos, I found my grace.
In the quiet, I reclaimed my power.

And in the quiet of her own making,
she discovered something new—
the power to speak her truth,
the courage to let go of the weight she never should have carried,
and the grace to rise without apology.

Grief Changed Me—So Did Grace

Because grace doesn't always whisper.
Sometimes, it demands to be heard.
It demands to breathe, to break, to rise.

You have that grace within you.
Let it speak.
Let it roar.
Let it set you free.

Grief Changed Me—So Did Grace

Because choosing grace also meant choosing truth—no matter how
much it hurt.

I chose to face myself fully—
to call judgment on my own reflection,
to stand in the wreckage without turning away.

I walked through death and rebirth,
confronted the demons of my past,
and endured the dark night of my soul.

It broke me open.
It tested everything soft within me.
But I made the choice to heal—
not halfway, but wholly—
from the inside out.

I faced the shadows not to become bitter,
but to learn how to stay tender in a world
that tried to harden me.

Because true healing isn't just surviving the pain—
it's choosing not to let it steal your light.

Grief Changed Me—So Did Grace

The path ahead was unknown—
filled with uncertainty and fear.
But for the first time in a long while,
she felt a quiet resolve to trust herself…
and the journey she was on.

Grief Changed Me—So Did Grace

There were days she didn't feel strong—
when just getting out of bed was its own kind of victory.

But she no longer saw those moments as weakness.
She saw them as proof she was still trying.
She saw them as truth.

Because strength isn't always loud.
It's not always bold or unbreakable.

Sometimes, it's the quiet decision to keep going,
to whisper, "I'll try again tomorrow,"
to rise even when your heart feels too heavy to carry.

She had learned that even in her most fragile moments,
there was power.

A softer kind of strength—
the kind born in the pauses between the pain,
that honors the quiet spaces,
and knows the smallest acts of grace
can carry you farther than you ever imagined.

Grief Changed Me—So Did Grace

And even when her strength wavered,
grace remained.

Grace reminded her:
you don't have to heal perfectly.

You just have to keep going—
imperfectly,
honestly,
and with love.

Grief Changed Me—So Did Grace

Grace isn't just for the grand gestures
or life-changing decisions.

It's for the small, unspoken choices—
the quiet moments when you choose to keep moving.

It's for the mornings when you wake up
still carrying the weight of yesterday.

It's for the days when you let yourself rest without guilt.

It's for the moments when you choose to forgive yourself
for the things you didn't know,
the choices you couldn't have seen coming.

It's for every time you show up for yourself,
even when the world feels heavy.

Grief Changed Me—So Did Grace

At some point, you realize
people won't always show up the way you hoped.
And that realization stings—
but it also sets you free.

You stop waiting for apologies that never come.
You stop shrinking yourself to fit into spaces
that were never meant to hold your healing.

You learn to offer yourself
the same loyalty you once begged from others.

And slowly, quietly,
you begin to understand:
your wholeness was never meant to depend
on someone else's presence.

Grief Changed Me—So Did Grace

Some will be absent.
Some will disappoint.
Letting go of expectations becomes part of moving forward.

It's a painful surrender…
but it clears the path for strength to rise within you.

And in that surrender,
you find something unexpected—freedom.
The freedom to reclaim your peace.
The freedom to choose who you allow into your heart.
The freedom to stop carrying the weight of unmet expectations.

Grief Changed Me—So Did Grace

And perhaps most importantly,
the freedom to be fully present in your own life—
to find joy again without hesitation,
to open your heart to new connections,
and to let the echoes of grief settle into a quieter place.

You are not defined by who stayed or who left,
but by the love you continue to carry,
and the life you continue to create.

Grief Changed Me—So Did Grace

And in that freedom,
you begin to rise.

Even with a heart still healing,
you rise.

Grief Changed Me—So Did Grace

She never relied on others to show up.
She learned to be her own comfort,
her own strength,
her own peace.

She chose grace for herself,
even when it felt undeserved.
She gave herself the same compassion
she had once offered to others.

Grief Changed Me—So Did Grace

She always showed up for herself,
even when the world felt too heavy.
She became her own safe place—
not just for herself, but for her children.

She became the steady heartbeat
in their uncertain world—
the one who held them close,
even when the weight felt unbearable.

She became the soft place to land,
the steady hand to reach for,
the quiet strength that never left,
even when the world felt unbearable.

**You have the choice to let go of all people, places and things that
no longer serve you on your new journey.**

Grief Changed Me—So Did Grace

She carried herself through the darkest days,
not because it was easy,
but because it was necessary.
Because grace isn't just something you offer others—
it's something you must learn to give yourself.

Grief Changed Me—So Did Grace

And if you're in that place right now—
where the days feel impossibly long,
where grace feels like a distant memory—
know this:

It's okay to have days when you struggle to stand.
Days when the weight feels too heavy,
when the whispers of doubt grow too loud,
when all you can do is hold on.

Even then, you are still moving.
Even then, you are still choosing to rise.

Grace isn't about never breaking.
It's about finding the courage to keep going,
even when the cracks start to show.

Grief Changed Me—So Did Grace

Grace is not just a whisper in the chaos—
it's the quiet strength to stand,
even when your knees feel weak.

It's the gentle reminder
that you can be both brave and broken,
both resilient and tender.

It's the choice to speak kindly to yourself,
to forgive the days that felt too hard,
and to honor the small, quiet ways
you keep moving forward.

Grief Changed Me—So Did Grace

She became her own anchor in the storm.
Her own shoulder to lean on.
Her own soft place to land when the world grew too heavy.
Her own peace.

She learned to sit with her own silence,
to hold herself in the emptiest moments.
To whisper her own name
with the same tenderness she once reserved for others.

And that changed everything.

Grief Changed Me—So Did Grace

That's when the real healing began—
when she became her own safe place.

She realized she didn't need to wait
for someone to catch her.

She was learning to catch herself.
To stand in her own strength.
To offer herself the grace to fall and rise again.

And that, too, was a kind of grace.

Grief Changed Me—So Did Grace

She realized that in choosing herself,
she was choosing life again.

She was choosing to breathe,
to stand,
to heal.

And that choice was a quiet revolution all its own.

Grief Changed Me—So Did Grace

You are not just surviving.

You are becoming someone who will rise again—
stronger,
softer,
more rooted than ever before.

Grief Changed Me—So Did Grace

In time, this healing will become yours to own.
A quiet, deeply personal journey
that only you can define.

Your strength will rise from within—
not from outside approval,
but from trusting your own journey.

Grief Changed Me—So Did Grace

Others may not understand your healing.
They're not meant to.

This journey is yours.
Yours to walk.
Yours to define.

Grief Changed Me—So Did Grace

It's a path that demands courage.
It asks you to step forward,
even when the way is unclear.

To hold your head high,
even when the weight of loss pulls you down.

To keep choosing life,
even when it feels easier to stay in the shadows.

Grief Changed Me—So Did Grace

And in each of these choices,
you find pieces of yourself you thought were lost.

You reclaim parts of your heart
that grief tried to silence.

You remember that even on the hardest days,
you are still becoming.

Grief Changed Me—So Did Grace

You are not just a survivor.
You are a warrior of quiet resilience.

And that, too, is a kind of grace.

Grief Changed Me—So Did Grace

You are the author of your story.

Grace is what you give yourself
when the day feels too long,
when the silence feels too loud,
when you stumble through your own thoughts
and still choose to stand.

It's in the quiet, everyday acts of courage—
the decision to rise,
even when the path ahead is unclear.

Grief Changed Me—So Did Grace

And you alone will decide how it unfolds.
That's where the beauty of healing lives—
in the freedom to be both broken and whole,
both hurting and healing.

Grace lives in the sacred space
between who you were...
and who you're becoming.

It's the quiet courage to write new chapters,
to let go of old narratives,
to stand tall in the truth of your journey.

Grief Changed Me—So Did Grace

It's the strength to pick up the pen
when your hands are shaking,
to write your way out of the darkness,
to carve out a new beginning,
even when you can't see the end.

It's the quiet acceptance
that healing doesn't erase the past—
it weaves it into the fabric of who you are,
making you stronger,
wiser,
and more alive than before.

Grief Changed Me—So Did Grace

And as you write,
you'll find that each line,
each word,
each choice to keep moving forward,
is a testament to the resilience
that has always lived within you.

Grief Changed Me—So Did Grace

She stood tall, head held high,
and reminded herself:
I am not my tragedy.
I am not just my grief.
I am not only my loss.

No—she was more than that.

She was a mother.
Resilient.
Strong.
Still passionate about life.

She began embracing her new life—
with grace,
with joy,
with peace.

She let go of everything—
and everyone—
that no longer served her healing.

Not from anger.
From peace.

She chose to release the weight
that was never hers to carry.
To set down the expectations of others.
To make room for the life she deserved.

She reclaimed her power.
She reclaimed her voice.
She reclaimed herself.

Grief Changed Me—So Did Grace

One morning, as the house slowly stirred awake,
I caught a glimpse of my own reflection in the bathroom mirror.
For the first time in a long while,
I looked at the woman staring back at me and saw more than just loss.

I saw strength.
I saw survival.
I saw someone who had walked through fire and come out the other
side,
not unscathed, but unbroken.

And in that moment,
I chose to see myself as whole—
not just as someone who had endured,
but as someone who was still rising.

And that, too, was a kind of grace.

Grief Changed Me—So Did Grace

And as she continued forward,
she realized that grace wasn't a single moment,
but a thousand small ones—
a choice made again and again.

It was in the way she still reached for the light,
even when the shadows lingered.
In the way she still chose to breathe,
even when the air felt heavy.

It was in the quiet resilience of a heart that had learned
not just to survive,
but to rise.

Grief Changed Me—So Did Grace

She was ready to make new memories with her children—
moments that honored the past,
but didn't live in it.

They carried their angel with them—
quietly, lovingly—
every step forward.

She had learned:
when your whole world burns down,
what remains are your memories,
your family,
and the choices you make next.

Grief Changed Me—So Did Grace

So how will you end your day today?
With grace?
With rest?
With hope?

However it looks—
let it be yours.

There is no wrong way to heal.
Your grace is your own.
Your timing is sacred.

Grief Changed Me—So Did Grace

This isn't about perfection.
It's about progress.

It's about finding your way through the quiet moments,
the hesitant steps,
the long, aching pauses
where growth slowly takes root.

It's about choosing to keep moving—
no matter how small the step—
offering yourself grace in the quiet moments
when doubt feels heavy.

Grief Changed Me—So Did Grace

It's about proving to yourself that you are still here.
That you are becoming whole.
That you are choosing to live.
To breathe.
To hope.

Grief Changed Me—So Did Grace

And in those small, quiet choices,
you are building a life that honors the love you still carry.

Grief Changed Me—So Did Grace

A life that moves forward,
even when the past still whispers.

A life that rises,
even when the weight of loss lingers.

Because you are still here.
Still becoming.
Still worthy of the grace you give yourself.

Grief Changed Me—So Did Grace

She kept walking.
Not chasing healing,
just choosing it—

again and again,
in a thousand quiet moments.

And that, too,
was a kind of grace.

It was in the way
she still reached for the light,
even when the shadows lingered.

In the way she still chose to breathe,
even when the air felt heavy.

It was in the quiet resilience
of a heart that had learned
not just to survive,
but to rise.

Grief Changed Me—So Did Grace

Because even in the quiet,
even in the small, unspoken moments,
she was still finding her way back to herself.

And that, too, was a kind of grace—
not a single moment,
but a thousand small ones,
gathered quietly in the spaces where her strength was born.

Grief Changed Me—So Did Grace

— "Grace means that all of your mistakes now serve a purpose instead of serving shame." — Brené Brown

Grief Changed Me—So Did Grace

Journaling your Thoughts

What does grace mean to you in the context of grief?

Grief Changed Me—So Did Grace

Journaling your Thoughts

Have you experienced any unexpected moments of grace during your darkest days?

Grief Changed Me—So Did Grace

When Faith Meets Grief

Grief tests everything—even faith.
There were moments I felt abandoned by God.
Moments I cried out and heard nothing back.
And there were other moments—quiet, unexpected—
when I felt Him sitting beside me in the silence.

My faith didn't take away the pain.
It didn't fix the loss.
But it gave me something to hold onto
when the world gave me nothing at all.

It reminded me that love endures.
That I am not walking this road alone.
That grace doesn't always shout—it often whispers.

And when I couldn't pray, I just breathed.
Some days, that was holy enough.

Grief Changed Me—So Did Grace

7 STILL CARRYING YOU

Grief doesn't disappear.
It transforms—quietly reshaping itself to live beside me.
Some days, it's heavy—a weight I can't set down.
Other days, it hums in the background—quietly present, but no longer defining me.
No matter how it shifts, I carry it differently now.
With unspoken resilience.
With a gentle resolve.
Woven into who I've become—stitched into the very fiber of my being.
And with it, I carry you.

Grief Changed Me—So Did Grace

Everything I thought I knew—
about myself,
my life,
and my future—
came burning down in a way I couldn't begin to process.

Now, I carry you differently.
In the steady courage I discovered within myself.
In the way I keep showing up.
In the way I show up for others.
In the tightness that still grips my chest when your name comes up
unexpectedly.
In the way my heart skips when I hear someone else say your name—a
small, unexpected comfort that reminds me you're still here, still part of
my world.
In the way the silence in an empty room feels heavier, reminding me of
the weight of a life that once filled this space.
In the way my breath catches when a memory surfaces out of nowhere,
pulling me back to a time when you were still here.

Grief Changed Me—So Did Grace

I carry you in the small, ordinary moments.
In the way I still set the table for one too many,
in the way I catch myself reaching for my phone to tell you something
you would have loved.

In the smell of fresh cut grass that reminds me of lazy summer days,
in the sound of your favorite song coming on the radio,
in the way the sunsets hits the deck on quiet evenings,
reminding me of the life we built together.

I carry you in the quiet, unspoken habits I can't quite let go of—
the way I still glance at your side of the bed,
half-expecting to see you there,
the way I still wear your old sweatshirt on chilly nights,
because it feels like a hug when the world feels too big.

Grief Changed Me—So Did Grace

There will be days when you feel like you're falling apart,
when the memories feel more like wounds than comfort.
That's okay.
Even in those moments, you are still carrying them.
You are still moving forward.

Grief changes the way you move through the world.
It shapes the way you pause in doorways,
the way you sit in familiar chairs,
the way you breathe through the quiet moments.
It's in the way you still whisper their name in an empty room,
the way you still hold their presence close,
even when the world has moved on.

Grief Changed Me—So Did Grace

I carry you in the softness I've learned to offer myself.
In the way I catch myself reaching for your hand when I'm
driving,
when the road feels both endless and too short.
In the way I still picture you in the driver's seat, barefoot,
leaning over with a grin as we pulled up to a fast food window.
You never wore shoes when you didn't have to get out of the
car—a simple, cherished memory that still brings a quiet smile.

Grief Changed Me—So Did Grace

You are in the grace I've found—
the quiet, unspoken permission to keep living,
to keep moving,
to keep loving.
Grace—a steady courage that holds both the ache of what's been lost
and the hope of what remains.
In the love that didn't end.
In the story that keeps unfolding—
even though it looks nothing like I imagined.

Grief Changed Me—So Did Grace

This isn't just my story.
It's ours.

These memories—they are anchors.
Reminders that love stretches beyond space and time.
That your presence still surrounds me,
quietly guiding me through this life.

I used to think healing meant letting go.
But no one tells you how unnatural that feels.
Letting go once felt like forgetting.
And I couldn't bear that thought.

Grief Changed Me—So Did Grace

Now I know—
healing doesn't mean letting go.
It means learning to carry the love differently.

Not as a wound,
but as a quiet, enduring bond of grace—
one that weaves through every part of who I am now,
binding the broken pieces,
holding together the fragments,
and reminding me that even in the deepest pain,
there is strength.

It's the quiet comfort of still speaking your name.
The soft smile that crosses my lips
when I hear a song you once loved.
It's in the way I still carry your laughter,
the way I still hold your memory,
not as something I've lost,
but as something I will always carry.

Because this isn't just my story.
It's ours.
And it always will be.

Grief Changed Me—So Did Grace

I've walked through the fire.
I've screamed into the silence.
And still—
I've danced in the kitchen.
I've laughed with my children.
I've filled these once-cold walls—
our sanctuary—
with warmth,
with laughter,
with memories that carry your name.

Grief Changed Me—So Did Grace

I hear your voice in the way you used to sing a song,
each chord a reminder of the quiet moments that shaped our lives.
I see your hands on the strings,
the way you leaned into the music,
lost in a melody that still echoes in my heart.

I see your smile in the faces of our children,
the way their chin curves just like yours.
I feel your presence in the unguarded moments that still catch
me by surprise—
in the way they laugh, argue and in the way they love.

I've stood in the sunlight.
I've let hope find me again.

These are not contradictions.
They are proof that grief and peace can coexist—
different,
but not separate.
Carried together,
just like love and loss.

Grief Changed Me—So Did Grace

If you're reading this,
I want you to know—
you're not alone in your grief.
And you won't be alone in your healing, either.

Somehow, despite it all,
we keep moving.
We carry them with us,
their love a quiet, unspoken guide,
an unseen thread that weaves through our days.

Grief didn't end your story.
It simply rewrote the way you carry it—
not as a weight,
but as a bond,
a quiet strength that holds you steady
even as the world shifts around you.

In the way you still pause in the doorway of a quiet room.
In the way you still catch yourself looking for their smile in the faces
around you,
letting the memories wash over you.
In the way you hold their memory close when the house falls silent,
reminding yourself that even in the stillness, their presence lingers.

Grief Changed Me—So Did Grace

To the ones still carrying them,
I want you to know—
you are not alone.

You carry them in the small, quiet moments.
In the way you still reach for their presence,
even when you know they're gone.
In the way you still catch yourself whispering their name,
as if the wind might somehow carry it to them.
In the way their memory slips into your thoughts
without warning,
tugging at the threads of your heart.

Grief Changed Me—So Did Grace

You carry them in the choices you make,
in the dreams you still dare to have,
in the way you keep showing up for yourself
even when the weight of loss feels unbearable.

You carry them in the way you still find the strength
to let love in,
to let hope grow,
to let life slowly, quietly take root again.

And when you feel the ache,
when the memories feel like too much,
remember this—
you are not just what you've lost.
You are what you've chosen to carry forward.
The love,
the lessons,
the quiet, unbreakable courage
that has brought you this far.

Grief Changed Me—So Did Grace

You are still becoming,
still rising,
still finding your way,
even through the hardest days.

And that is something beautiful.
That is something worth holding onto.
Because you are still carrying them—
and that love,
that unspoken, enduring connection,
is a legacy all its own.

Grief Changed Me—So Did Grace

You carry them forward—
in every breath,
every choice,
every quiet act of courage.

In the way you still whisper a memory to them,
as if they might somehow hear it.
In the way their presence lingers in unspoken echoes,
filling the empty spaces between every heartbeat.

In the way their influence lingers in the smallest moments—
the way you reach for their advice when a decision feels heavy
or catch yourself repeating their favorite phrases without even thinking.
In the way you carry their quiet strength into the hardest days,
finding comfort in the habits they left behind.

In the dreams you still dare to have,
in the plans you make for a future that now includes their memory.

In the small, everyday choices that honor both the ache of their
absence
and the quiet strength their love still gives you.

In the way you choose to keep loving,
living,
and becoming,
even when the weight of the loss feels too heavy to bear.

Grief Changed Me—So Did Grace

And maybe the greatest miracle of all—
is that you're still becoming,
even now.

Not despite the loss,
but because of it.

Because you chose to keep building,
keep dreaming,
keep loving,
even when the world felt shattered.

Because the love never left—it just found a new way to stay.

Perhaps this is the quiet triumph—
not just that you survived the loss,
but that you're still growing, evolving,
even now.

Grief Changed Me—So Did Grace

Because grace never left—
it just found a new way to stay.
It became the strength to rise from the ashes,
the gentle courage to dance in the kitchen,
the resilience to fill empty rooms with warmth once again.

It became the murmur in the stillness,
the warmth in a long drive,
the reminder that you are still here—
not just surviving,
but becoming someone who will thrive again.

And that is the legacy you carry—
more than just their memory,
but the enduring bond of grace that binds you,
even now,
to the person you're becoming.

Because through it all,
you chose to keep living,
to keep loving,
to keep becoming.
And that is a triumph all its own.

Grief Changed Me—So Did Grace

— "What is grief, if not love persevering?" — WandaVision

Grief Changed Me—So Did Grace

Journaling your Thoughts

If you could write a letter to the one you lost today, what would you want to say?

Grief Changed Me—So Did Grace

Journaling your Thoughts

What part of them still lives on in you—in your choices, your values, or your growth?

Grief Changed Me—So Did Grace

The World Kept Spinning

One of the hardest parts of grief isn't just what you lost—it's how quickly the world expects you to move on from it.

Bills still had to be paid. Waking up to take care of the kids, getting the kids off to school, the house, the lawn.

But everything had changed.

The firsts after loss—birthdays, anniversaries, holidays—felt unbearable.

You try to smile through cake and candles, but the ache is louder than the laughter.

Even in public, I learned to hold my breath when people asked how I was doing.

Sometimes I said "I'm okay" just to end the conversation.

What they didn't see were the nights I stood in the bathroom, holding back tears, wondering how I made it through the day without falling apart.

Grief doesn't follow a calendar. It doesn't care what day it is.

But I kept showing up anyway. Quietly. Unapologetically.

For my kids. For myself. For the life I was still allowed to live.

Grief Changed Me—So Did Grace

Grief Changed Me—So Did Grace

The Grief Timeline *(Emotionally, Not Chronologically)*

Storm – The moment everything changed

Silence – Numbness. Fog. Stillness

Ache – Where the memories live

Survival – Small steps forward

Strength – The moments you didn't think you could do

Surrender – Letting go of what you can't control

Grace – Being kind to yourself in the middle of the ache

Becoming – Not the old you. A deeper, wiser, softer one

Grief Changed Me—So Did Grace

A Note for You, Reader

You don't need to be unbroken to be whole.
Your pain doesn't disqualify you from peace.
Your past doesn't prevent your healing.

This story—mine, and perhaps yours—
is a testament to the strength it takes to keep going,
even when the way forward feels uncertain.

As you turn these final pages, I want you to know that healing isn't a
straight path.
It's messy, unpredictable, and often full of setbacks.
Some days will feel lighter.
Some will feel impossibly heavy.
And that's okay.

What matters is that you keep moving.
Keep choosing hope.
Keep offering yourself the grace you so freely give to others.

Grief Changed Me—So Did Grace

You may not be the same person you were before,
but that doesn't mean you aren't whole.
You are still becoming, still growing, still finding your way.
You are worthy of love, even on the days you feel unworthy.
You are worthy of peace, even on the days you feel broken.

Remember, you are not alone.
The grief you carry is a part of your story,
but it does not define you.
You are more than the pain you've endured.
You are stronger than you know,
and you are capable of healing—even when it feels impossible.

You are not just surviving.
You are becoming the person you were always meant to be—
stronger, more compassionate, and more alive than you ever thought
possible.

Grief may have shattered the life you once knew,
but it has also made space for the new you—
someone who can walk through the world with more empathy,
more wisdom, and a heart full of love.

Grief Changed Me—So Did Grace

Take your time.
Be kind to yourself.
And know that, as you continue on your journey,
there is always room for grace, for love, and for light.

Maybe one day, your story will be the reason someone else doesn't give
up.

And if no one else tells you today—
I'm proud of you for thriving.
I'm proud of you for showing up.
I'm proud of you for continuing to breathe through the breaking.

You are not alone.

Grief Changed Me—So Did Grace

ABOUT THE AUTHOR

Delilah Klug is a mother, writer, author, and resilient soul who knows the heartbreak of losing a spouse and the beauty of rising through it. Her journey through grief began with unbearable silence—and slowly unfolded into a quiet act of survival through words.

What started as a private release became a path to healing—not just for herself, but for others walking through the fire of loss. Delilah writes with raw honesty and deep compassion, creating space for sorrow, truth, and hope to exist side by side.

Her words are both a mirror and a lifeline, reminding readers that grief doesn't mean you're broken—only that you've loved deeply.

She lives with her children, whose laughter continues to be her light, and writes to honor both her past and the future she is still creating—one page at a time.

Grief Changed Me—So Did Grace

Reflection & Resources

Grief is not a path you follow in order. It's a terrain you move through—sometimes forward, sometimes backward, and often in circles. There's no right way to grieve. But here are a few gentle prompts to help you explore your own journey:
Journal Prompts

What part of your grief feels the heaviest right now?

When do you feel closest to the one you lost?

What would you say to them if you had one more moment?

What strength have you discovered in yourself since your loss?

What does healing look like for you—not in theory, but today?

When You Need Support, you don't have to do this alone. Consider:

Talking to a grief counselor or therapist
Joining a support group (local or online)

Connecting with others through books, art, or letters
Gentle Resources

Option B by Sheryl Sandberg and Adam Grant

It's OK That You're Not OK by Megan Devine
GriefShare (griefshare.org)

The Dougy Center (dougy.org — for grieving children and families)
Refuge in Grief (refugeingrief.com)

Grief Changed Me—So Did Grace

Dear Younger Me,

You won't see this coming.
It will hurt more than anything you've ever known.
You'll wonder how you're supposed to keep going.
You'll scream into pillows and fall asleep in tears.
But you will rise.

You'll raise two beautiful children through your grief.
You'll hold them when they cry,
and they'll hold you when you can't speak.
You'll find strength in the softest moments,
and grace when you least expect it.

You'll write your pain into purpose.
You'll find others who carry their own losses—
and your words will remind them they're not alone.

You'll never stop missing him.
But one day, you'll laugh without guilt.
Smile without breaking.

And you'll be proud of how far you've come.

Love,
Me

Grief Changed Me—So Did Grace

A Thank You to My Readers

To you—

Thank you for holding these pages in your hands.
Thank you for sitting with the hard moments,
for allowing my story to touch yours,
and for trusting your own heart enough to keep going.

Thank you for holding space for grief,
for seeking grace,
and for finding the courage to keep going.

Whether you read this through tears or quiet reflection,
know that your presence here means everything to me.
Your courage to walk through grief,
to feel deeply,
and to seek healing is no small thing.

You are not alone—
not in your sorrow,
not in your hope,
and not in the quiet transformation unfolding within you.

May these words remind you that even in your darkest moments,
you are never alone.

From one grieving heart to another, thank you.
For reading.
For showing up.
For being part of this story now, too.

With all my heart,
Delilah

Grief Changed Me—So Did Grace

Still Becoming

I carried the silence, the storm, and the sorrow.
I walked through the fire—then through the ash.
I learned to breathe again, softer this time.
I didn't just survive.
I became.

And I'm still becoming.
With love beside me.
With grace within me.
With light ahead of me.

Grief Changed Me—So Did Grace